HOPELESSNESS

Published 2020 by the87press
The 87 Press LTD
87 Stonecot Hill
Sutton
Surrey
SM3 9HJ
www.the87press.com

ISBN: 978-1-9164774-9-0

Cover art by Eloise Walker
Cover design: Stanislava Stoilova [www.sdesign.graphics]

Who will wipe this blood off us, He said
    that boils the ground
He ricocheted the night. Swallow. Again, even more.
Chewing on the pelvic floor, the life that creaks away below
    who shudders in the light.
Softly, some obliteration slipped into the air,
    and what is without confidence? Passion,
    passion, passion; softly taken, beaten in
    its world of intensive make,
    the shuddered climate open, and getting steadily worse...

I wake up, and I close my eyes.
I push my head through the window.
The city tenderly roars. I close up
the slits of your neck. I pull my head back,
and you stand there up to your ankles in soil,
dripping wet, completely gone. I go to the window
to cancel my softening eyes.
Clouds tear across the leaking moon.
A body is pulled from the world.
My body. Your bodies. Ankle deep
in a grave filled with water, singing the boat song
together. We are standing in the half light,
in the dark, and we are singing
like cancelled moons under the leaking sky,
just above the ground,
frantic with wires and tubes. We can say nothing.
We feel nothing. We are singing because we are dead.
The moon and stars are also dead.
Our dead bodies sing for the dead.
We hold dead bodies in our
arms, our mouths. We are creaking
and ghostly in the half light
and at dawn we part again, and go out to our lives.
We stare along the shore. A terrible sound in the throat.
What are we that we sing these bodies, in basements,
in the bellies of boats, streets and shelters. We are heavy
and silent and still, like a grave.

I gather my things and pad to the window.
There is a hard blank wall, an indissoluble connection.
I listen for when the night will stop,
when your face appears in the leaking light,
in the light that is coming in the morning.

PRELUDE

(after Sappho)

I am lying in a dead body under the dead light on the water.
You are the distance. As I lie here in my body
in the warm dead sea, you are the distance,
the light at the top of the water, the arriving and the leaving.
I stare across the field to the buildings. So many lives
inside that place they move in the light and hide in the dark,
the field inside the dream, where I climbed into the ground
through layers of wires and posts, down into the soil
to find your still living body, having been there, down
in the earth all this time, and we began to climb up
through layers of pipes and posts,
                         to move into the light of the field.

You are still dead, asleep in soil and I wonder who thinks
of your name, goodbye until paradise, until we are
inside the wires. I touch the surface of the water.
We have sat quietly and suffered the violence. Lost
our interior lives. My eyes are against the water.
My body is beneath you, being slowly deadened,
its attrition. The water has covered my body and I am lying
dead in the water. What a frenzy in my breast raged and by
what cure to be assuaged, what gentle youth I would allure
whom in my haunted heart secure, who does this fractured
life subdue, tell me water, tell me who. You may live
                     between the sand and the salt and the breath.

We woke inside the dead water. We were scared... like any
newly born baby opening our eyes to a gigantic glow — we
lived in the dead water, our dead bodies glowed, we were
frightened... every knock, every word. We realised our panic
was minute compared to the panic of the mirrors,
and it flashed: We were invincible... because we were
everybody. We held our bodies together in the dead
of the sea. It is a life of attrition I live to refuse, under
the cover of the dead water in my dead body I hold you
to myself, you are still older than I am. I believe that you are

still moving through the world and through time,
through this slow dead water, so beautiful and calm,
the surface that I touch with my palm.
                              I stopped being living for you.

And this will be your food, the salt of the water.
And this will be your air, my blood and my skin.
And this will be your light, the pulse of my chest.
And this will be your sleep, the sleep of my body.
Look up, so much beauty, look into the ground.
Squint with me, into the middle distance, so far
back and I am dragging you out of the ground.
The escape is corroded. Your overnight balance.
We go out of our minds and tear the skin from fish
I am lying beside you forever and speaking this.
You are moving close again, handing me an open paper bag.
I long for your heart to move. It is still.
The ground is somewhere, gone. Wind tears
the scaffold sheets. But I can barely speak. I lift your body
out of the water and begin to walk, holding you in my arms,
barely speakable. Please fall out of the dead ground. So far
away, and into the hungry earth. I stretched and lifted you
                              into the dried up air.

The birds are silent (while you remain), in the woods
a complete silence of birds. The beauty of the skies I hold
you there, Come then, I pray, grant me surcease from
sorrow. We are no mercenaries, shaking children unjust
in the soil, we are destroyed at inception, dead in the soil,
dead in the water, the water is dead, dead in the sockets,
dead in the chest. We are dead in the water and the soil. Salt
will be our food. Kill the soil and the water,
I want you to live again. These are my last words
for you, the salt and the water, the birth and the death.
Come away from dying, come and stare at me again.

Grant the sound to cease from sorrow,
quickly the light will follow.
I watch the lives are destroyed.

Give you limbs and teeth, life after life,
up from the soil, up to the air, limbs and a chest
and eyes to stare and the peeling deadened water
                    and the mouth of the ground.

Of barely seen, hardly noticed, you were in grey and red,
some yellow and the sun in your glass. Would I breathe
at you, strobing yellow, grey flecks of red would my dreams
haunt me your climbing figure dangling from the sand
and salt stained in the sun on the white paper day
I stare down into the bag there's nothing in it the colours
are flotsam we'd array love arrests my heart it has destroyed
the mind is over is all that is left O, slipping contrast love
                    robbed my heart.

I love to fall asleep, but I fall asleep to you. I am robbed
of sleep and robbed from the heart. We lurch up together
in the dirty water like wooden deckchairs. I think your chest
is moving, or peeling away from the earth.
There will be eleven more summers, you said.
And my hand moved slowly across the soil.
I am near to screaming for you, because you bob in the soil
like a collapsed deckchair, close the sky and a little
like the light that is coming to touch the sky,
and I do not expect your chest to move, nor for your eyes
to gently fall open, nor for the ground to give you back,
nor for my breath, for paradise singled down to a tiny fleck
of yellow in a sea of gray, or a few red bands.
                    But I can hear your voice.

I am Tube, the vivisectionist. The sky tonight
is an absolute banger. I do not expect to touch the sky,
but it bangs and it aches like fuck. He said to me, Sappho,
you sick little vermin. I said, "but you're married.
                    Just like a cop".

A bit of your voice, a tiny glint of how you would speak
with a little creak fleck of yellow, red and tongue
the glass, but where we were or trace of you in a carpark

as I sat there alone, like the soil. Sometimes buried
to me or sometimes that one time so alive and climbing
back into the world, older and able to move
through wires and tubes in the ground. And what you do
to the heaving chest though never my eyes
dusted in soil and decomposed, just a piece of your light
                    seeping into the creaking air.

How the aching sky tugs the tiny chests from the ground.
I clench all of my teeth. Deep into the scaffold sheet howls
the cladding wind, paper and gold, grey or gray, two strips
of red, eleven new summers, I am the birth and the death
and the light that is coming, the hopeless stunted light
that is come to go again, lain against the water's top. Red
on red I am dead to hope I know not what to do:
I have two minds. In doubt I am, I have two minds,
one is grey, the other a hopeless splash of yellow or gold
I know not what to do. With my two arms
I lift your tired body from the speechless ground,
so, like a child after its mother, I flutter like a scaffold
in the tearing wind. The eyes of my head scan tenderly
left to right, the eyes in the sockets of my body in the water
stare up at the soil through the salt to your chest.
To me thou didst seem a small and ungraceful sea.

Now that we are allowed on the grass will you not speak.
I will not speak. Your voice with a tiny creak.
You drank in the water forever, every single piece
of the water inside you, but you shall ever lie dead;
it feels as though everyone has forgotten, that I alone burn
for you to live, that tiny blotch of colour by the gate
of the car park. Now we are allowed to go onto the grass
you wander unnoticed even through death folding
 into the shadows and fixed to the gloom
where memory seeps away like the water
                    you drink in forever.

I clench my wet fists, shot up in colour.
The killing of a wave in the colours

of the field, the rain is done the sun is come.
Circuits and the stars about the grey moon
throw down their red beauty.
I know one day that you will come,
that your madness will step aboard the world,
do not try to save me, stay in my arms.
                    Do not save me.

Down in the leaves press to my cheek
the grassy eyes of the hollow bare ground.
The motions of soil from the motions of the ground
from the motions of water from the motions of your chest
from the motions of the water from the motions
of the ground to the motions of the soil;
I stand chest deep in your grave, my eyes gently scream
in the rain. Why were the ground why were the chest
why were the indicants of the field. Now we go
are allowed to the grass and the grass for our feet
is the life in the arc, we are falling and moaning,
smiling and sharing, a prelude to taking you into the earth.
I am stood in your grave neck deep,
trying to dry out the last of my eyes.
They will not come dry. They are like the dead water
that won't stop pouring into your mouth.
The never ending drinking of the dead water
and the never stopping fleck of yellow or gold
the grey and the grain of the floor, that pillar,
the yellow tree in the corner, the birth and the death,
the pillar, upside down, jutting from the hard grey ground,
slowly lilting in the warm cool water,
                            holding in a trance to our chests.

Sweet victims in the soil
chewing salt,
I am so glad we're laid out onto the grass like this,
best to a tender front may I liken you
to the quiet water's top
there was no other, no other sound but your quiet chest
please come back to the grass,

stir not the pebbles, I am standing in a grave,
            up to my shins, and the rain has stopped.

We are alone, with blushes and gently darting eyes;
our kind voices reach up to incredible colour
in the air, in the water, the bulb and the gaping tube,
gathering chests and holding in the longing swell
as soil to grey against red to the last fleck of yellow or gold
creaking into the dead grey light
on the water, the light of your life pouring out
                to the haunted and emptied shore.

HOPELESSNESS

Who will be the lady,
  Who will be the lord,
When we are ruled
  By the love of another? Tell me,
Who will be the lady,
  Who will be the lord,
In the light that is coming
  In the morning.

Perdutamente
Con vibrato ridicolo

I've tended a song to sing to you with,
to hold my mouth to your teeth and mutter
        to each a tiny song;
        to gather in a swell of trails
a thousand tiny Volvos sliding through your neck;
        a song of tenderness rippling round the trees,
        of banishment, a curtailed species
bungeed in the face of its harness;
how I would hold you in a limbless clot
        just above the water;
where we could lay, curled in our chests.

Hold me like the impending Suggs, the silence touch
to touch our skin, and in this spasm just above the bone
poison in the ear, deluged in silence the train it
wakes up
        disappointed lean on your exit
        no windows level
        the walls
pay to crouch contorted on the floor
        take it back
        be ephemeral.

        No term of grit
        fellating gentlest whirring meadow
        British analytics
        British fisheries
to the Elizabeth Line I gurgle
God accept my tiny quivering
ephemera:
        "Tell me *I am* the Universe."
Trip me for the first time to the woods,
the crook, earth has fallen off.
Since you ruined my life I destined
        it should be.
And what is sovereignty?

17

Look, innate rota; so what is that
cultural loss we are rolled up in
Angels, deference, bodies, soils, salts, wires, tubes
            to see what saying is
            brave hearted shit for tongue
            beats you over and over the stars
which hail the night who wakes
to pay £54.40 crunched to the
British floor of the British speck
with its British conditioning (air)

            the distant glimmering engram,
            technocrats guess who's gone in
                        their pants again!
Jack Monroe is a snowflake thrown across the air
brave and missing fingers cracked in plastic hail,
Diane Abbott is a snowflake smashed
to a clot of loss CN Lester is a snowflake
Water is a snowflake. Toilet is a snowflake
Air is a snowflake.
Care is a snowflake.
            Something in this world that seems to fall open.
I build my haunted lists to crescendo in this moment:
A call to the radio thrashing the world
my meanings tooled up and remorseless
or just to make this joke: "My grandparent
thinks that Suggs is creeping towards the door,
but it might be encroaching madness."
            Everything's covered
in severance. When my ssofftt voiccce broke over the soft joke
phone radio in to you and whispered:
"My grandparent lies, softly by the door
            I wait there like Suggs as the trouble impends
            likebreached madness she thinks I'm coming up
            to the door, my long Suggs' fingers pierce
the impending darkness and make a small soffft noise."
Wipe out the surface /
a box of mouths
I think it's time for a reasoned debate:

18

A local man, a sofftt father, stop cutting
to a beautiful daughter
standing up to little curled up plastic fingers.
being wasted out to death in heapes of soily
tubes like hands, those plastic gloves
who come alive to open into graves
that death switch on a gorgeous life.
A local beautiful falling man.
A dead in watered surface shrine.
A toddler dressed as a gamekeeper wafts
          onto the creaking balcony
"floccinaucinihilipilification." Nothing. And again:
"floccinaucinihilipilification, floccinaucinihilipilification!"
For a moment the perfection trembles
inside a vacated meadow.
          I pray to God my tiny
          voiceless soul where could you
have gone, no life, anti inhabiter, former sea mammal.
It is now here are the Useful Terms:
          Living as part of a terror.
          Net Wt./ Poids net "our soft
          power unrivaled."
          I love you too much for this soft fingered heart
                    crush it. Nail it. No mad.
          A string of lanterns is hanging in the rain
          outside a portacabin by Finsbury Park.
It hurts us all. Accept: The country; you are listening,
I don't for one second imagine
but my friends are beginning to die
I love you too much, destroyed,
          what a thing to say in a civilised node
like, we are the slow and cutting detritus of our lives.
          Batten is the cruciate attached to a mouth
          made of bins already an anachronism,
          a fading remit of broken life
          chewing its own dead face like a lamprey on fire:
You can't say that:
You've a nice flat
          buy a fucking hat

sing a shit song
        have a shit time
electro swing is a personal favourite of mine.
There were no Morris Dancers
        before 1844.
        Where did it come from.
Where did everything come from.
...You burned Ryanair's 20% to €319m, Generation ID,
        sent down in that fucking room with
your eyes my tiny burgled fingers snap off
        stuck in rubber not correctly fitted a penny a glove
the trigger passionately grouped on the police
        what it means to do your own life back to me.
So the service user now has the notion of returning.
To travel at least along portions of the life
which are not occluded by engrams,
like that lifeless man I wrench the lid
to collude the agitated flume tired fan gripped to clear for
once for blessed weather, taut
to nail after nail up gradually dying. I said
instead as I itched herself forward;
a diminution. Ali Dawah. Lucy Brown.
        Charlotte Church is a snowflake.
Petition: Universities: Suspend Social Justice in Universities.
What seems died out to have happened,
ribs take a long time to heal O' Brien
It's an analogy to fatherhood
his umpteenth urethra, melancholia,
        universal melancholia.
Since you ruined my whole life
that is its ruined homeland,
Christ is in us all. Unnameable Mercy.
Take it back. This is Jack. Jack wants it back.
Jack wants it back... Open your mouth. Creasing and glue.
        Hanging. Back.
        National Service. Back.
Be like Jack and send it all back.
You woke me up and ruined my life
my bedside aching through the night

your eyelids flashed with rage and pain
that couldn't later half sustain
the agonies I kept pressed down
for years, just below the ground,
and now, as though to open up,
corrupt myself and touch the cup.

Another morning burrowed in
the Autumn who destroyed my skin
and once again I stared at you
and wondered what our life could do.

All too soon a voice appeared
like Dennis Potter's daemon, smeared
my face familiar with his
reallocated torment vis-
à-vis a perfect daughter, mine
society has left behind;
so what then for a cloud like me
when only daemons can I see
and yet won't name a single one
incase they say my sense has gone.

And so instead I supplement
a silverback who heaven sent
to lie for me and make us strong
slaughter you for to be wrong.
I am not that fucking stupid
you don't see the ages pass
before begins the horrid task

of hate in me like quills from cupid.
Make me vengeful strong and gallant
ringing out the lamprey's pain
switch my heart back off again
until the blame becomes apparent.
Even then just switch the blame
so long as all of some disdain
makes anybody else aberrant.

Daemons sore from me at night
to exercise my speeche's right
to have its cancellation sway
like Morris Dancers stuck in May,
my speech conducts my thoughts to move
my hands into the comfy groove
of never knowing always being:
Mindfulness, this time with feeling.

By daybreak I'd have signalled through to you
and quip "James it is you myself" through to you on radio
"James it is is me myself. We are as towers in the air
like collapsing Dibnahs
morphing into your nostalgia for a hatred ever present
but languishing in a past existence tended and reformed to
bare the weight of unnameable passion. Speak"
He passed me on the stairs. We fell into quiet.
Good night my darling. He said. Put you into my bed.
I said. So they slammed across the meadow.
I am illness and speed. He said. Then let's
look forward. You said. Let's never abandon.
He said. Let's flume and gesture. It said. Let's.
But before she could finish. He said. Am I right
to be thinking. Am I right in thinking
that you. I'll tell you this once and once only,
I am greater than my senses but still desire
to die. Then everything gets a little. He said.
Either you all die or some of you live.
Fixated on the electricity riser between the training room
and the office proper. Fixated on passion like a damaged
proctor. Fixated headless in the meadow. Dying for the GRU.
Winded by the OPCW. Splattered into splitting processing
by ISIL. Confounded into action by the DFLA. A bruised
identity floating like a bag of dusty remains in the poisoned
carpark. I go there and scream to the IC for help.
IC! "Answer! Answer! We go to graves!"
A screen crackles into light: A speaker in its soffft corners:
Con Adenoidi
– I'm not on benefits young man. So these days I prefer

Democrats. I wouldn't vote Conservative again. Not so
keen on Conservatives
anymore.
(Crackles)
– Scuse me... Scuse me...
– Fuck sake. Why don't you do us all a favour
and commit harakiri.
– Well if you don't vote you can't moan can you young man?
You have to vote if you want to have a say in politics and
I'm trying to explain the difference so you can understand.

      His body with hellish compressions.
      People begin to speak. Begin to sour
      the ludicrous softness of a grandparent shedding its
      in the inferenced seismic generational
      consternation fucks gives birth. Blame
      was the mobilised antidote
      to real confrontation as if you see it and at once
      invent it. Be like Jack. This is Jack.
      Be like Jack. Live in the moment.
      Jack doesn't suffer. Suffering is fake. Be like Jack.
Jack is from glue.
– Hello James you twat I'd like to talk about fish.
– They lined up solemn outside the Church Hall
      performed the Analytics.
You fail to account for Narodnaya Volya;
A pulp of alienations compressed into a public
vector of coerced and abused pain,
tendered and racked into singulars as each pivots to
next despair, exorcised into a set of siphons;
a vulgus graft angled over the crest of a pivot
into hatred in entire human life or siphoned back
into whichever bodies seem the most precarious,
      turned out to face a terrified wall,
      its own pain mirrored
      in the graft and in the plaster,
curled up in an abstraction called "your culture and values."
– I am a Local Costello - Hater of Paedophiles. For the last
few months my daughter's been softly tugging on my arm
asking about higher education. Obviously I'm a very busy

man what with leafleting and the little plastic gloves they use cost a penny each but we could be waste them on or at maybe ten pounds a glove! etc. For a while I paid it little attention thinking this was a soft phase which would pass her by and maybe leave her feeling really stupid when it all turns out to be make believe. Unbeknownst to me, however, she'd sent off some applications. I was not hurt. She received three unconditional offers which I was bloody well expected to be proud about when the little rubber fingers not fit properly a disgrace at ten pounds each a glove while people are lying on beds. So I did my research. I'd heard all about these 'Universities', snowflake replicators. Parsons Extruded Remoaners. I checked the list of courses available and to my surprise there wasn't a single one listed as a 'Social Justice' course. Perhaps Sargon's petition had worked. Next I checked to see if there were any Paedos there. Paedos, which I hate. There were two convicted staff members. Doddery old white professors. Not much of a grooming gang if you ask me. Reader I ignored them. For once I felt my conception softly inch itself towards the door like grandparent fingers unwrapping my not hurt exact-ly, but fingers, peeling them out of the little plastic gloves they have at ten p... My daughter. My deal. My taxes. I left myself at the door and flew back home with the leaflets. The sun let itself shiver through the curtain. My heart rate monitor. No daughter of mine's goi...

Can we go now? It's boiling in here.
Can we go? I don't want this. Gone. No. Itch.
Shut the fuck up about your pain. There is no pain.
    /
If I hear one word from you about your 'pain'
    /
(you are a snowflake) It'll tear everything down.
You don't want everything down do you?
You don't want everything falling
like the pit in your neck.
                  You want it back.
You want it back. You want it all back.

Put these in your mouth:
The nationalities of maintenance workers
the way we used to play in the street before
the vanishing; want my kids out like the film
to equate to love back. Want that back. Want parkas
and taking a joke back. Want meat on Christmas day.
Want the Birch. Want monetary modesty
for the upper middle, debit croutons
for the halfway dispossessed, want jail screws
non sexually. Want handwriting hard on burning skins
and lessons proper taught and cold porridge back.
Want a thump supper from the Sergeant Major
and cold limp cabbage for water, 'Allo 'Allo!
was a documentary; Want fireside teacakes
and neatly soundtracked Anne Boleyn
washing clothes by pulverised hand,
lives through the mangle
and asleep in the furnace to ignore one another
forever back. Want ignoring each other forever back
won't somebody think of the fish?
Want the ocean stink before us
to take out the fish and eat the fucking things
ourselves – want trad jazz aquatics and amateur dramatics.
Want open lips and Danny Boyle death ceremonial
shoestring gristle in the teeth and step on step on
and string the bastards up back.
Want Paedos swinging from the skies
and traitors pouring their guts life minerals
onto eager hungry hands in the cooling towers at Drax.
Want wanting everything back back.
Want the self before all this back.
That's not what I said and how dare you,
want an idea of how we were before they came and tried
to make the loss back. Step on. Step on. Step on.
Slowly down to die, Oh!. Cooling now, step on. Step on.
Who is this. That is coming... Step on. What. The IC. Gone.
Step on step on step on. This is Jack. Jack wants it back. Be
like Jack and send it all back.Can we go now? It hurts us
all. The room is cramped shut and I am on the floor on all

eight of my legs. What do you want
me to feel, IC? Get 'em on board - I'll call it in.
EXT. // SKIES OVER MOUNTAIN RANGE // DAY //
The commuter plane struggles over snow-capped
mountains.
INT. MAIN CABIN, COMMUTER PLANE //
CONTINUOUS //
I am stuck to this world. It shudders uncomfortably in its
harness.
The three Hooded Men kneel by the cargo door, hand-
cuffed.
      feels more like:
Okay, okay, cool it sunshine.
The lights are on and everyone's home.
No. I won't have it. Not like this.
– First one to talk gets to stay on my aircraft. (Cocks
weapon.) So,
who paid you to grab Doctor Pavel?
The gravel outside is splitting to wire.
(The Soldiers grab Hooded Man 2, hang him out the door.)
– Tell me about Bane. Why does he wear the mask?
...
Lot of loyalty for a hired gun.
– Or perhaps he's wondering why someone would shoot a
man
before throwing him out of a plane.
– At least you can talk. Who are you?
– It doesn't matter who we are. What matters is our plan.
...
No one cared who I was until I put on the mask.
We are nothing, are the dirt beneath your feet.
– If I pull that off will you die?
– It would be extremely painful.
– You're a big guy...
– For you.
– Was being caught part of your plan?
– Of course. Dr. Paval refused our offer in favour of yours.
We have to find out what he told you.
– Nothing. I said nothing.

26

But we saw blood. We saw pleasure.
We saw the stars and I finally got around to making
that song to sing to you with:
But there's another gender we've heard of long ago.
Most rare to them that seek them, most dear to them that know
We may not go to uni, we may not graduate
But as long as they've got money, we'll marry boys we hate
And boy by boy and drunkenly our conquests will increase
After seven years of CLC, our suffering will cease.
I finally got through with my immaculately formed joke:
– My soft grandparent is worried that madness is creeping up
to their door softly tapping on the windows of her house,
encroaching their life to its nozzled end, when in fact the
culprit is Suggs.

>Spirit of my silence I can hear you…
>(But I'm afraid to be near you
>And I don't know where to begin)

Life has tired out
>I feel I have aged
grief thins the sky around your head. The air in the air
purely also nothing. Hold me like a limp grandparent the
wind destroys
in your arms like the impending Suggs: Tell lies for me.
Destroy for me. Vanquish the paranoid schizoids
the anti-psychiatrists, musicians and Gramscians
tear the face from Bookmarks; birth me in the smugness
of ripe wire to deny the dents you birth. Compress me
like fuel pull their eyes out of storage
punch and discredit me from helicopters
cradle me in your soft fingers like ten Suggs
a glove and every grandparent's soft madness, Suggs me like
a polished weeping life how rarely tears come,
so we hung in the blossom like snowflakes
inside in utter defeat, your arms pulled back on.
My stupid life dared in moonlight O, softest grandpaero
tapping gently at the folding neurotic windows
when the person Suggs softly called out to the ambulance:
How do such horrific violent outcomes sublimate
and depth charge the horizon. Because of,

not in spite until my mind is gone bring back hanging
in the blossom like snowflakes.
God, please don't let them take my mind.
Toss me back for the first time to the shelter
the hollow, life has fallen silent since you left,
an insult to still say "life", where've you gone I miss so
many things
but that one glint, the pretend unnameable –
            all of life's detritus floats by it.

How can it be said at all mind is going
            somewhere else valium somehow illegal, how
to tender out this song for you to your teeth,
to the soft water,
            of its perfect negative deal.
Late meat flakes
            pepper the Sorostriction
customised you,
            why your fury
is at all
            record levels
we were left by the last
            better times
white
            death
at the
            borders.

Sing too little
            in the light that is coming
better to celebrate
            howl with the wolves
the passion of the footsoldier;
            the vanguard.

And once more, I stepped
onto the balcony and threw my dreams
            across the leaking air, traces banged the moon
damaged, but you gone

no longer has access.
You, the howl clots... Conservative Woman
Christian Institute, Generation Identity in the carpark,
        outside Berlin in the Spring
but if you were there
        or for what they must be beaten
because they dare not
        at night the groans and sobbing. I want to say
a man's garden was dug up, there was supposed to be
a machine gun in it. Nothing was found. To squeeze
a confession they beat him. His corpse was brought back
to the hospital. His body had boot marks on the stomach
        and fist sized holes in the back. The official
cause of death? Dysentery.
        Now filibuster.
Trip me up for the first time to the woods,
the crook, life has fallen off, you left me
to mangle so many dead coda, asleep in the crematorium
windows where life's one dream one time
        floats off by.
Internicide, flat amounts to you
        terrifying person
this song for you to your teeth tremble
to the soft water,
        dispirited person.
Better meat flakes
        kiss all over, like I could meet you
there, I would mend you too
        your fury taken onto me, again, taken onto
you at all. Fuck off
        beached insurgent, Drill makes
locked in step, step on
        took her purse with a child there were
white
        borders, not enough if you ask
too late for that
        in the light that is coming
in the morning
        howl with the dead blood. Describe it to you

the passion of dead blood wolves
    for the endless insistent vanguard
onto the balcony and threw myself down over and over...
        ...but you are gone and I want to speak to you
now,
and the world you're out of
        access to, so I access my light,
relieved to miss
us pouring down Queen's Road in the morning
by the Community Base
        in July I am there with you in a tiny light
It is all miniscule now
        and beaten through,
because we are afraid, nightmarish
        and if I could ever forget about
that winter, one amongst many
dead face mimics, turning up to the ground
will obsess this lonely method of wind
reflective nuance, until I too am no access
        and fist sized.

I will break my back.
I am in a grey room with damp paint hanging off
        the high walls. There is a permanent gag in it.
        Now one last communique:
Reported in tomorrow's broadcast taking
responsibility for for the outcome
        that they /   takes place.
That me loving you, a Suggsual
        journey to total ownage
of the light
        that is coming in the morning,
having won though that winning will
be nothing more than nebulous self light
on a terminal course to the long knives next year perhaps
but we see together near this encroaching door
how much love you can reasonably and responsibly do.
Rather than ascending to any life at all
to love You, whatever it is you want to do,

and however you get there
take me home, my gorgeous fingers,
          terminal grandparting the waves bulge with
antenatal, correctional handbook indistinct
lives uncountable, we shall rise in the light
          that is coming.
After it, when the storm front dies
in the light that is come to snow down like fingers,
          the bare soft light in the morning, terrible music
          played beautifully, hoisted on a pole
          the Harvester flaps stiff against the cold East wind.

HOPELESSNESS

The kye's come hyem, but I see not me hinny
The kye's come hyem, but I see not me bairn
I'd rather loss all the kye than loss me hinny
I'd rather loss all the kye than loss me bairn

The Hard is almost still today.
I lie here in the light.
Who is this who is coming?
The sky is sloping gray.

There is a another emptied sky
where bodies fall to ash,
and in a twitching swell
an open neck, to death, at night.

The final sounds are clipped away, synced and paused...
the peeled sky.
You hear a glass crack,

...the hard is still, the stink of mud, little holes
in the ground.

I have longed to know what you are,
for years, how nothing happens.

Somewhere you have never been,

I stare down into the hole.

Your body is lying there up to its knees.
A heap of mouldy ceilings.

We fell quiet, our gullet, mast-lamps, outflow.

I itched with the flame...

And I have left the floor.

Your body is lying there up to its knees.
A heap of mouldy ceilings.

We fell quiet, our gullet, mast-lamps, outflow.

I itched with the flame...

And I have left the floor.

These are the last few pages.

Somewhere you have never been, a meadow

and near to it this arid hum of wires.

Smashed flowers.

Chewing at a wounded floor,

a song to sing to you with.

I stood under a moulding head.
A cluttered dusk of bodies,
stretched out;
bodies, fungus.

Kaybar and Diane,
Church Street
buried in the light.

I was a botched reason, hung above,
would never once more be,
and so as I am kneeled now so

blankly from my home.
You are Nothing hurt
builds in, going to the end of being.

A mind softly danced.
This, against the cold is,
rattling proxy necks.

so to live a simpler life...

When I die I'll be stuffed by Twydall.

Sugar for sugar, gloss for gloss.

You look into your mirror.

Who is this light, is coming.

There is a sense of a new scale.

I smelled a corpse in the woods.

I sensed a corpse in the woods;
a thing that may not be said.

I rot and calibrate.

I rot and calibrate, the vision.
Driving into the bed,
so let me arrange the things. A sky and a piping,

so the gorge is split to hell.

We spilled the day on the grass;
we are allowed to sit.
They let us play,

so fall into the blades above the world.

To say dust.

To dare to speak with his mouth.

And now I stand untethered...

Years across the road.

Our choiceless rain, the car park, farther.

Pascoe, Kaybar,
we can't go on like this;
a cellular
bulge in a clot
make peace not
love not
ah!

The air is very bad for you, who radiates for surcharge.

"La Vie, l'Amour, la Mort."

We are blissful on the grass.
Perimeter metal spikes.

Fighting out your own eyes. "Are you proud or dead?"

Pascoe, cut from the grass.

A hateful inseminate. Parlour games.

And if hard water runs the winter into my skin

the scratching to blood informs the course of work

as work has failed, is attached to the sway

of the seasons up to 591,
a clumsy attempt
to another town

yellow and tender the pool of your eyes
the skipping leaps of your buried head

My spores, my spore,
my announcement pure;
strong, I am, and determined.
I am a life in the service lifts
I form, from a lilting dream
in the rising and falling dreadstate
I am new, made up and trusting.

In the Light that is
Light
Dendrite disimpaction:

Lubed in phlogiston,
it dangles from its arms...

Oh so now we form a stoop
with our little feet apart
and we bend and stretch
and we hold the form

the woods who swallowed
the birds, those stymied
fragile ghosts.

So saw their love part
from the door by gasp

taken as she was and stood
at the stoop of the shop as I lit

and the smell is sweet
the drawer of plugs

Before the muster you were beaten.
A tiny hidden shoe. A glue, a thin,
I am going to punch the fuck out of his eyes.
a song called imagine
in a tree where a Pascoe climbs
I am lying like life in a dead-sea grave
and squaring off threats, the storm is coming.
In the distance you ghost is burned in the hand
in an imaginary tree, will we grave and tide?
We were caught in the coconut fumes from the hand.
You're heard, but far too gone to clear.

sleep in heavenly peace...

The spider has spoken
hir softness.

The foreheads stretch away.
To overcome is everything

never a law nor a clump of eyes
my ankles deep in your grave.

She goes to retribution

the crocodile incinerates.

A howl breaks free of your lips and into the air.
We ate in a strange congress. After the food the candles
ache. You go out of the door to howl,
the night is choking. I am there in the shock of an age
with you, unable to properly know. Somewhere
you have never been. A meadow. Close to it the smell
of no light, the howl who echoes softly.
It is a slow and silent day. We are straddled
into systems.

I have burned his crocodile.

I hurt for his hurt was mine was

all of his eyes punched out.

It is breaking outside of us
our interests are lost.
I will tear out your eyes
against my own.

And though it is outside
for breaking
on our lips and
the burning light,

a song who haunts to the bones.

In the light that is coming in the morning...

The point
is bursting in her cage.
The meat is soft
and boiled.
The skin is Luger
shrapnel.
The stains
are done and coupled.
A tiny person
wrapped in gray
with flecks of red
and yellow.
Gone into
the silent mud,
and speak
to her forever.

And so I on I on and on to meet and dance and sweat and pop to when must on for out I go and on and live and laugh and love I love I laugh I live I on for on to live to laugh to leak as inch for scurvy on to sick and move like meat to pop and swing and hopeless on to never bolt I on I live and laugh and love like hope oh dead sad wart and network job would put this body popped and sex the price and stop and on and on and on and on and drop we make we live new songs we list we build we hopeless spit are gone to live we laugh we thought I pray and on I can and on I won't I will I will I can a problem put it back it all back on to suck like ground I forceless on to chant the names incant the naught as if to stand but not to move would not to wheel and on as no so when in silt miasma on to laugh to love to force for us would weight be taught and measured flat would off and you become avail.

On, insistent choice but nothing shrouded base to live on off; scoured and hit and burnt to plastics on convulsed not set on fire; leakproof skin of burning mermaids on would shot or corpse you back. To how inert I blank the pivot loss of self is stained up sick would tackle workplace false and on in scaline fucking air to weed the tense of sun that peels the back-skin shut pour an inciser through the eye the eye the needle Jesus cup his face with iron lungs scratched and on and on and on and grilled to putty not yourself so if so eyes not just propped up but shed like living, laughing, love! And on and on and on and on wake up you fucking ankle deep wake up my life is spread with dreaming clusters up her aching chest. Neck down to soil I punch and on and on to ground the will that was as not as ever not and never gained for else could be. Closing down the sandy woodlands hard and sucked the outflow decks but sunk in cloying mud far down is gone or dragged back out not see.

Back one inch and move away to cry out based against the sky would not forsee or trust retention gave or shudderedinyourgravemyfiststomossthatachesthesoilwho composts tender in the woods or scatters up in nitrous

phloem what at best a glint to know how then have crushed
these human birds that weld and on again but no, trusted
sick to make to shape up greedy smears the outlet's heart,
my sea as love itself is buried don't hold back your hand
stripped bare. I dint or laugh and love the world there is
another failed sky so cut wake up to soil and drip not
here but if so to not oh too, as well as fur has damped
to kill and edge with no will further pressed pneumatic
pretext stains the crossed out measure not again. I can I
will unceasing power that surges not solutions grape and
parcel tiny hooks for feet and cage I popped apart and on
and cracked and hopped for life but broke to meat there
too will see both you and you as evermore to fuck will
go in cancelled logic no or no and either no then cycle do
to, more, with apathy or wasted outflow tired the deck
who crumpled through to light so not but gone erode to
tide will take as with so gone you were and are not here
but how and on as if to broken no inside but not you,
ever here no will no not so when not ever here so not
now gone to you forever, left, and thereabout you turn
so never more to no again drawn out in filthy dreams.

Mud to mud let up and rise to throat your foot for burial.
To drop like heads reformed and on or twitch away an eye.
For you return to rise in mud the throat I shit to sing. As
if you fucking clutch the wooden roof so wet appears. All
too meant rotates and falls to live and laugh and love and
on and on and on and on and love and live and lilt in fire.

And shall we pray again, my love? To who? To God. That's
wrong. Then how. To start. Our help in ages past. The lift is
sinking down. I am going now. I am going to let go of you.
Don't let go. Please hold on. To the gate. To the gate. All the
days of our lives. In green. In red. In gray. No more. And
on. Hold tight. I hear the bells. I fall. The lift. I am. The lift
I am your help and lift and sink. To no avail. And on. There
is. You are. I go. You stay now, go. You wait. Yes? Yes.
Wait. No. I must hold. Leave not. Fuck you. Solid state. In
here. Poke it. Stuff your eye. I hope. You hope. You long

alone. Change! Change for one, for all, for us. Where goes?
I guess. Guess better, hope not, on and if to where go you
so on would if you fall great down like sink and lift slope
back into the leaking sky where one or all too, I have be but
soon come pass and back, for soft, at least, to blink away
your dream then back I lift and leak to come replacement
said oh smile at me if holding hands to make us hurt the air
is thin and change not come it not does come to who those
wait as if a cryssalis of us were too much light of change
today, and on and on and on and on and live to laugh with
you for love would shrink like necks passed out and back
again you hear it screaching night outside where change
that is not comes and splits our stupid heads back off, that
change, that much would well accord you gentle love my
spirit on will lock out my of your sweet head too much, too
kind, will change not graft where else the head I shot off you
was pouring thoughts I made them up, so what, get fucked,
like thoughts can do, so not, wry out, my vested shot.

Get lifted out of grave where sea won't go then
lantern back the message good, or vellum is so done with
you that not to think it not go back but back and back
and on and love to live and laugh and love and on will
in so early daybreak lurch like spluttered vomit, you as
well! Pascoe! Hear not crocodile you hold that sweet
toy in your arms go back and down in leaking lift cor-
rode the empty sky of you place more to more and on as
though you were not thinking I get that, and I get you
that more would come to me to make it yours again.

Wrench that stifled grass right down your egging throat
in yellow light, so scratching sharp as barbed I made it
senseless put back on and shit in streams uphill dragged
there by dogs a naked grey and red. No! Soft grand and
bottomed husk of person there, asleep, there is another
kinder sky that softly trilled our bones. Cancel back to
infinite the breaking chord you hand lift from the sinking
leaking bone of sky that shreds the chord so always known
you see it happen look away like hopeless daisies boys and

girls the sky is shredding up from leaking chord and glue today for you that never will go see again and on and on and on, to blanket out there is another cancelled air that twists your murky throat back up it goes to hopeless pieces in your mouth, the cruelest joy. Come out your graves you leaking spirits aching in our hopeless throats the sky that screams the sea back down to stain the emptied shore.

HOPELESSNESS

Who will wipe this blood off us, He said
    that boils the ground
He ricocheted the night. Swallow. Again, even more.
Chewing on the pelvic floor, the life that creaks away below
    who shudders in the light.
Softly, some obliteration slipped into the air,
    and what is without confidence? Passion,
    passion, passion; softly taken, beaten in
    its world of intensive make,
    the shuddered climate open, and getting steadily worse...

We lay down to die in the strangled grass. You looked
at me I looked at you. The sea was turbid and still.
Echoes of lives moved through the buildings.
I sat by a desk. You were helping me up,
but I had to be helping myself.

A cricket popped in her cage. I said
"from my chair." I thought. "I could communicate
from here, with my mouth, I could shout,
or I could use a phone or a pen. I could sign."

Silence hung in the wake of the world.
Private words I wasn't allowed.
I said "from my cellar. I could speak from an apple,"
and felt myself move a little; up into the quiet field;
an empty space, a carpark all tamped down in concrete.
Where have you gone?
Life has been so… something… since you left.
A scorn to still say "life." The walls shift a little
and wobble into line. And eight miles away
a clutch of people shouting, every flattened week,
the flotsam of the movements;
a process is botched. I am holding the cans
and the tube has come loose
from the tape at the incision. Spite
is the sound. There is no place,
and I have the past, lying in a trough. You sang my heart
is not convinced. My eyes were snapped awake.
A freezing bellow of wind
the long march through the carpark
to the cluster in yellow, echoing ghosts of a meadow
in a carpark, in a hall in a county in some
counties in a county by a carpark in a Strict and Particular
Baptist church by a car park inside a Strict
and Particular Baptist church
dying to return, my own Galeed,
to the floating mouth of the shore, who
accelerates yet still remains austere.
I could motion in a box, in a field, on a sofa,

in a chain, in a nozzle, in a bed, from a leaf, to a stone,
from a bolt to a gluey hand in cuts or to a blue / green
light where just above the car park in the sky that turns
the tarmacinto grasses, mourning you in LEDs, lamps drop
like wildflowers on the sea to kill the day, making your
best choices sensible, maggoty, diluted and in four new
locations: Grace Church, Vineyard... something... that
something... I will never forget suspended in space or air I
am lit and gleaming in the flowers my soft dead
body in the long warm grass, swish and smile up to blank
him off, Papillon LEDs reforming into foam. The tide turns
back, the hard is still, I come here to stare in the icy brine;
I could communicate from here, here and here. I use my
finger in my head, eye and tube, clumsily pushing it back
in the wound tearing at the bandages which gave their
hours to bleed me, who only want to do it now sluice back
through hard retention. Pain, and little plastic gloves. Take
you through the engram; by any quiet mechanism. The bed
sheet was red. The carpet was grey. The lamp was antique.
The pain was so... no. The bed sheet
was red. The window was clear. The meadow was there.
The eye has quit.

"... by any quiet mechanism,"
"Sorry, what?"
"We're going to try and attach the tube again now, the tube,
okay."
Lying in the lonely bed blinking and sighing, moving
gently onto a side and then another. There will be no
sleeping. There are thoughts. There is the blunt light and
smells. This room is a mistake, they think. They lie in their
bed. You are sent back to bed, back to the wide mind,
narrow down the tube. In a lit up park or field He presses
you dead and open, flat out, what are you.
Knowing. Transcript in motor by dead acute or rile. In a
cleft something I will never that memory held or arrested in
clot, coined and pushed to the pressure of testimony. Will
not forgive will not let up. May Chang flowers. "Tell

me." Across the new gaping meadow you are going on a
madness. A fennec stumbles in the war. Her hands and feet
scrambled like coffins. You are disruptive. Decaying.
Amounting to hidden excess. Scrub the road.
There is grass, beneath grass, soil, beneath soil,
nozzle, tube, wire, rubber, pulverised categories pulped into
meanings pushed into tubes, pushed into their wound,
cleaned and sent back. You tell the meadow "I did the things
that girls did, that... something... I can, or will... will never
forget, arrested? In space?" Constantly warring to recount,
stumbling into the wide open field... There is a ping-pong
table in a corner. A gulping crack like a voice sunk down. In
the middle of your dozing mind, a quiche. The men wear no
ties. Two of the women wear headscarves. A man is speak-
ing to the small assembly. His name is Richard Bennett. The
talk entitled 'Catholic Mysticism and the Emerging Church'.
I have been listening to the talk. It is dry and the children are
forced to sit in it. I have gone to leave the hall and walk out to
find myself in a larger hall of the same dimensions. The same
contents, even Richard Bennett giving a talk entitled 'Catho-
lic Mysticism and the Emerging Church - Reexamined', with
a tiny hall in the corner: A Strict and Particular Madness in
the home counties. Tiny in the larger hall: A Strict and
Particular Baptist Church in the home counties housing
a Strict and Particular Baptist Church in the home counties.
Outside of here are the home counties. In here the church
and inside it the church. Both in the home counties. Gently,
very slowly hollowed out.
...

Somewhere you have never been. A meadow
near to it and the balmy stench.
Summer pollen like snow, polder of the afterglow,
and you are flooded with joy in the pasture,
connected to, and the motion of the swaying grass
feeling your heart in your chest
taking in the gasses, scanning back the meadow,
connected to but not always, you going there
and walking in the lapping breeze.

Joyous light of late afternoon; not surprised
by it; swift birds swoop as if dropped
and catch back onto the warm rise
the ground sends up to the air connected
and swirl into brilliance, fully defiant
and as with the air the crickets
somewhere you have never been
are staring in a way that you have never stared,
all five of the eyes fixed points connected
to the optic globes of brain gazing in love
at the femur with its coarse hairs each
a dapple of complex hooks you have never felt
as this in the meadow, the mantis, not ideal,
perched by the kiss of a flower you long
and lift up, connected as you were then
to a primal longing for peace too easily shattered.

It is a scarlet day in a place you've never been
with your eyes closed, another layer of brick
and then another then some boards
and plaster then the hauntings of a place
filled up with the echoes of people
who are coming, who is this, standing outside,
making up the pastoral imagining
shaking your head, you refuse to use the word 'it',
you shake your head and nod your head.
You go to work and nod you go
home and shake, you sometimes shake in silence or cry out
past the field and into the pumping room where there is a
pipe touched by a person and it is always the one who goes to
care for you. Madly nodding your head. The pipe unblocks
and comes into you. You and many others, the same pipe,
always the same room with the human you shake when you
go home, where it is different, a different layer. The people at
rest you think of and don't think of; it moves around in your
eyes and the eyes of the unit according to where it needs to
be at work and at home it is always moving just beyond the
point of sight, which is annoying. Blasted away and out in
the meadow, in the deep dream state you pollen the horizon,

I am, we, you, the whole of the world walking alone in your
thirties through the meadow gently congratulating yourself, a
distant figure who is coming, slightly annoying, not the worst,
and when this beauty flies into the eyes you are younger again
and again shedding away all that pollen from the windscreen
where the spores fly off to the meadows and arable fields,
so tired that you'd like to die, which I mustn't do, you once
told me, held your head into the field's near pass, the copse
the babble of water distronictoxaemia. To before, now and
after, straining in the light of the wall, light of the late day,
magnificent birds flung up sick when the tube of another
kind of engine, one to take things out of my stomach
unblocked and attached in this happy trail
of a burning myth extinct, and then fixed onto a word:
The meadow scratch you out of the window along the lawn
miles down to a fountain whose noise stretched through the
silent air you imagine it floats up to you.
The possibilities have pared down, which is nice,
and in the meadow, for a quiet life, the tube flaps gently in
the West wind (at last) and the carer,
who must have been the scratching
in the pumping room, irritating your view
of an empty distance is gone, so surely
unblocking this tube can't be so hard,
you mutter into the still and balmy air
as you begin to fiddle with the nozzle,
the breeze being light enough the tube rocks very slightly,
yet still it's not as simple as it might have been, for once.
Still though, nice day for it, 101 things a boy can do.
– Mr. Sergeant? Are you awake? There's a visitor to see you.
The tube swings around to look up. Just birds.
Flocks of patients and a sticky smell.
It is pollen. I'll do it! And true to form
the nozzle swings up to the energy
of the hand put there but this time the blockage moves
about thirty feet back down the tube
and not into you which is where you imagine
that it ought to be, that's how it works surely,
or else how would it? The primrose shines out.

Papilio machaon, Iphiclides podalirius, do you see? A few
paces on. Nymphalis antiopa. Never seen at all, the
Mourning Cloak, you call back. There is nobody behind
you. Then a tap on the shoulder, that I am fearful. I am
mixing a strange colour for you, filled with glue and wool.
Still undulating your grim mouth near the tube the nurse
yawns and falls out, watches as you labour at the nozzle:
Blood falls luridly out of you and allows herself to laugh,
once, very quietly; stage one emphysema. You go into the
museum. Grim for the elated stylus. A tap on the shoulder,
this time narrowly. And you turn around to see the figure
drift off into the noise. Is it a secret? When do you think
you will head here?

Things that could have been yours; a tangible derelict
stance, unbreakable oath, on the feelings of officers, the
distant tattoo, and why this corrupt image: Too much to
easily promise, surely, and as the district softly agrees to
itself the Meadow becomes a station in prayer, an oath to
the silos, abandoned slag heaps, unlistening feelings,
protecting the hobbies of the meadow. You can't just start
to work and expect everybody else to follow, to turn to
them and snarl at having started without stability. You can't
just expect love you have to earn it, snarling back at the
indolent precarious day by night workers pretending not to
be tired or in grief but for the £3.70 you are promised and
in fact you can't be in love not at the moment,
anything you amount to must contain a strategy,
like getting out of being forever beholden to loss.

As you become awake your arm falls over your body to
study the nozzle. The button on the side of it lights the dis-
play. A message that says "As this is near the limit, please
ensure you have enough available to pulse at the nozzle":
You fear the nozzle.

We had been in a fair and stable phase. When you were
younger you worked. Things have changed. What is
normal, being underpaid, not being paid, being paid
according to the perceived quality
of your work, qualitative awards
now drenched up to your throat in
sunlight in the teaming meadow, you're moved into the
home. Never me, you muttered. Have you done enough to
be paid? Your mouth drips open.

Kaybar appears at the window.

Every morning they come in and hold onto your hands.
You can't read. Something is making you drop. You watch.
One day I will get up and dance, the nozzle glares but the
tube itself glares. You yourself glare into the hands you hold
singing a song from the forties that you were never in with
someone who has the same in common: Never having been
in the forties, in the light that is leak-proof scattered, the
pair of you fawnly lurching in song whose theme is against
loss both beholden to only loss, excruciatingly long,
and within it a quiet dignity called loss,
real loss, the kind that abstract loss can't know.
Hopeless loss without conditions. Radical hopeless loss
without the condition to move, no clause, just there; forever
at the mouth of the nozzle glaring out at the Mourning
Cloak in the meadow who sits maddeningly still,
tubes piping up their dark wings with blood.

As the life in you were confiscated, I walk on by a window.
There is a bed. The room is blissful cold. I stare for a second
and pass; meat compressed in double doors.
The bed is torn from the wall. The room is dead
in space. Dates of plaintive significance
reeled back in like tundra (July 2005, January to February
2007), without specialist access below the scheme of vision,
hidden instincts, who is coming (29th April, 21st June,
28th June and the 12th of July 2013). Flat out
in the garden, frozen in the warm grass a body lies
a damp protrusion, the earth giving it up.
The whole of the air is watching. Individuals gone
in chasmic meadows, fuel, and when they are sure that they
                                              are unseen,
completely alone they let themselves die; when they are sure
that nobody else is alive. Felt unable to work together,
connected to, gently, the greater tube, and its nozzle, alive,
                                    sobbing, connected
burnt, scrubbed through the voided grass,
to the cedars. The body had its arm hang off dragged
from the wreckage of the car. The soft jagged metal
sinks in the balmy grass you look back,
who would have thought, you think.
What would Gone have thought. Gone would shake
their head. Gone in absence is better. Gone is cured:
Not here.Gone beyond action, to pure being:
Is brave. Gone is finished. But being in Gone is more than
action; the action of being Gone is being gone.
The tube whimpers from under the ground,
troubles the soil and pokes through.
You stare down into the tube,
past the headstone, past the gate, past the empty tanks.
The tube follows your gaze, knows you down to the root.
The tube is like a root. You scratch your head.
The tube scratches their head. Their head is the cap
on the nozzle. It is pink and grim. The nozzle feels as
though its purpose has been sabotaged. The closer you get
the less time you have to react. Yield yourself to the ground.
There is not a light this who is coming?

The tube flaps deftly up to your face:
From where could you communicate. From my wheel.
From my sky. From my gum. My illiminature. A chthonic
mouth fills my mouth. The air tilts into the floor of the
meadow like harsh glue. There are zero choices. You may
have zero. Yawning into the air. Thank you for choosing
zero. Thank you for gluing your yellow body to zero. You
are given zero. Hopefully zero will begin to rise. Rise in the
light, the light that is coming, the light that's fucking coming
in the mo-orning!
The shivering tube glimmers wet and static
/
Tell me about sinking away. There is a horribly
                                    expansive courtyard
in a convent. I've been to it. I go there and there is nobody.
Someone is coming towards me. Do you feel afraid?
Yes. Thinking about your body in an ankle deep grave
in the sea. How is your grave ankle deep in the sea.
A plastic glove in the graceless capacity sky.

Step on, step on, and so the sky it heaves away. Look up my
love. Open your eyes. Here is the kinder sky! Officer, there's a
spider on you. My eyes are filled with chthonic dust the same
as in your mouth. Sweat and tremble in disgust or clamp
the jawline shut. Pressed inside the corner of the carriage
out to freedom desperate for just one eye to blink on you in
kindness. He sipped contentedly. He buzzed lazily. He fell
asleep. ...The pollen went to work, starting a chain reaction
of atomic force ..."Then the rains came, imbedding the seeds
in the rich fertile, warm earth", officer. Oh slack and careless
meadow, hot soil and ripchord. I know that this is you: I am
on a train with a group of us going to some kind of ceremo-
ny: Says: Every single hole is just too deep to fill; echoes of a
life set out, but free; completely empty. Hopelessness inside
the life set out but empty headed, stretched into the partisans
of day that made permissiveness, don't tell me what to do
or else to let me loose and break my speech into the open
light, like death made free like life and speech, measured out
by choice, by rote to dredge up all the fuel that makes you

blunder what the free in speech like death has torn you out
from under: I am carrying a heavy but small cube of a
television. It is difficult. We arrive at the ceremonial site where
Ben explains to everyone that it is time for him to leave us.
Trumpet music crackles discordant through the trees.
He states his reasons and method,
and everybody in the clearing, so many of our friends,
begin to celebrate and agree to watch him do it,
so through his skin, through his ribs,

he holds his heart still and falls dead to the floor.
I am the only one who will scream out,
staring into his gently dead face, its colour fading away,
his kind eyes transfixed with the giddy lie
                                        of their departure.
In the open glade idiots dance for betterment. The IC cackles
                            in the cover of the brainless trees.
I am not stupid but am hopeless, officer.
Managed like a standard relapse the shape of a head drives
                                        into the wall
and is cracked up, for a fragile makeup, a gene said to be
tested filling the air with fallen trees, heating up the chip till
it cooks and pushes the atoms around the meadow. Cancer
clusters spoken out in half light. You could never lie here
safely again, still there is a kingdom for us in the pump room.
They take out your blood and give back your blood. I can
hear my voice singing in the fog. It is a wreck choosing to fin-
ish down into the silent sea, right at the end of the boatsong.
Once again I trace the skin inside my life, the skin is falling
off my face sing my neck in time to yours I will never stop my
eyes. You gathered them up in your arms.
The shape of a body, the length of a confession,
and as quiet as this dreaming field the hot sky forced down,
at length we spoke in the grass by the trees,
pathetic as a hole in the ground. Desperately I lie awake
and take my secret tablets, paranoia floods my heart
that someone is coming to stab me.
What did you do to make the door
of a young soul's house bolt up so hard?

Why not tell the morning with your crying
and come back to me. Going to prison makes the neck
inside your eyes go hard.
Stung in summer stretched inside
the rest of the tubular year,
each marked and put away. All out and nothing in.
Charged and out again. You just fall into its arms.
Relieved the loose soil and the grass, stupid at your feet.
Consequentially shut up. Frogmarched to the water
and put beneath it, raised up and down again,
the undulating pressures are the maddening,
are the hopeless flock of despair gathering up
in a cloud, dancing the air; and you stare up
from the water from the air from the water from the air,
the view undulates as pressure, and the birds in turn
mock and persuade. Cancel the men who stand around you
shouting on and on and on to sleet some new unpracticed
tears,
but who am I to say this. When you left our lives
you left a hole for hate to prize apart.
I woke up in the morning, my chest was shaking open
wanted to mourn the life went out that left a heart
inside the freezing woods.
Cut a certain speech away, the anxious knot that won't
obey
companions that blast it out, ignore that pattern reflex.
Do it again, only properly. You go under the water
and in a sarcastic voice gurgle up
at the stultified image called 'birds',
homeless bees and plastic foreshadow,
your pump room voice your gorgeous interior,
cresting chest, for how could love be...

A little hope flickers in the side of the eye.
Go from door to door, toil at the ground,
toil at the leaving, crisis part. Hacked incendiary.
Little or no motive. Varied cuttings.
Little segments of insect. Leftover skins.
Arms in a basket. Static negligence. Erratic fizzing.

And on and step on step on. Density. Copula.
                                        Obsessively aching.
Meadows. Plagues. Slow injury claims. Getting it done.
Solutions not problems. Back to work. Help to find support.
Abandoned construction. Paper cuts. Breathing in the water.
Being dragged to splinter. Masses in. Trellised plastics,
electricity riser, juncture, for the beetle's case in your skin.
Sucking and trenched, the gasp of field breath;
repellent: Unnatural. All these petty absolutions
breeze past our lips in the cool morning, gagging order.
Ink in every order, soft bodies, soft ink on paint.
We stare back agape to the meadow. The wonderful fields
of Europe, still dusted, drowned, from the recent trauma,
fast new derivatives, and the late of the trauma fade
in her finale, just now a cadence, a cricket pops, exploded
exoskeletal ombre, dragged almost to death,
compost, in this sweet aubade as you were,
shocked gorgeous by the boot to the mouth,
heavenly weather. Watched from my wished to be gone head
glued to your gone mouth as we kissed catastrophically,
the rain well-wrought this wall: Weirds broke it.
I said you said the nozzle gurgled the tube
in your sad hanging mouth or nozzle,
morning, coming, light, nowhere, stoop.

The healing winter behind us. Chlorinated meat.
Connect, connected to. What was in your head; lying there
dreaming in the tubes and machines, peeling from the wall,
conn to cross out the face, in colour emptied and forgotten,
th. This is for everyo... Cnnctd to remark in mould damage
simmering dbt This is for Everyo, mh rendered image: 20
New 'Operator' jobs, and is it cold. Did it hurt. Ghost, flesh
the horizon. Slowly down the spiral stairs, into the leaking
water, monobloc in design, what do I want from you. Sisterly
divisive. Lost to it, exquisite death, Else smiled in the break.
Of the horizon the healing weather exempt oh split and crack
in a manic fireguard, Article. 24. passes by, flawed,
for extension. The petty horizon in manic slow
is cold, basted, the EKL burner, forever in chlorine

extension, white to pale green, skin to cold healing, leet as rendered image, connected to, in extinct remark red mist dries cold in chlorine connect, spread in fathom and about hurt, in fingered yellow and shackled remnants more than five bodies. Our museum lilt, to a face in colour emptied, monobloc, emptied, sached, chlorine,
basted, clean and well. Oh fell to fireguards. Stoopid green aggression. Agitate as meat washed fell to healed fire and will persuade.

We are the extras in the carpark. Panic is expertly leveraged to a broken surface. You glare back at it, the stupid fonts and wallpaper. The glue in your throat on the phone. The tube spinning madly in the distance, unable to be attached now the experts have fled, fumbling glue fingers after it. You tear on your high vis and screech into the street. Death until the empty meadow seethes in chronic calm. Let me die into pieces. The expert zeitgeist chaos valve hums
the street to actionable contact, with you.
The cold healing winter
springs up, saying a rosary.
Squeezing dreams from a sewn up sky.
There are six challenges to complete,
you are in a vast decay, buildings blasted out,
bleed back in: where the waltzers are removed
and forgotten colours lazily switchback fistfuls in pits
and. This is for everyo... Keep a burning summit
in his balconette
for impact, crush, given, and collective. It was Plaster.
Bollard. People ask me how you are.

Tell me some more of your dreams, or if you can cut me
                                        open,
to be near again to the fires outside, or crisp and even snow.
An apparition at the empty beach. The beach is vast and
                                        dulled,
a cold concrete ridge miles adrift to tell your dreams
you and I are cold again. Aren't you suitably cold.
Drifting up to the empty shore it stared across the ice,
the ice stared across as sure as drift softy ensconced a photo
                                        light
the creaking chair in the corner. Floating out to you;
dream to hate again. Turn from the edge to the empty
                                        apparition,
not again. Currents tear to crystal but it stands there staring
                                        at me.
So far off the empty beach it terrifies my sleep
and still tread softly onto the water, climb away to the
                                        ground.
But if it should hear me... Sink this silt body mine,
what if that thing could hear me? At the shore the spite is
                                        bolstered,
what have I taken, when did it hear me? Only on this desert
                                        stay
and fold up. There's a small pipe stuck in the ground.
And spite glimmers in the resting sky, in your brains.

You lift up an inch of turf and glare in. It flickers like an air,
there across the edge from us, up to the spiteful fucking air,
there like a flame above the swirling sand. There is no flame
to my eyes who is this who is coming across my back, the
                                        eyes, behind
above in muck and toil the ground who is this
who is coming. Who a flame floats along the shore is.
This gentle oath to the ground an empty side in the water,
Your numb hands breathe, immobile, for days agape
beached to choice,
somebody come who is that, oh no. Stay by my sleep,
slow terror sleeps. Somebody hold the back that stands
against the distance

the first sheets are tearing down show us and gulp to the
distance.
And spite flaps in the air and I cry into my softened mouth
for only hope.

Folded in the lap extremely call across the site,
will reach out to trust with nothing,
clothed unclothed exceed to the bounds,
edge and riddled who is this, who is coming. Whose neck is
split
the beach expense; expressive straits turn into the day
what comes when slow death spits and dies away;
are slow spirits waiting in a quiet open world without an
ear to creak for?
If you're drugging me to rifts no crashing at the edge
or hands below the door, who is that what is coming.
Pinning the shoulder, hatred crumbled tile,
losse sheets let nothing end you permissions,
end you hanging loose please hold to, just until we're out
of this miniature false clutch. You must not toss my teeth
into the shuddering leaking twilight.

The foot is walking, the tiny world, take us up float back
into the soaking ground a little lift to take away the lives
that sent
it into the grave; I met with you there
across the ground, a speechless creak.
Leak and spread to the earth, care passed over to another,
no, the gone and slow creak sparsely, one alone against the
sky
who is it some slowly gone creaking echo of a shadow on
the beach.
Scatter life over this cold and echoed climate, a tangible
shake
tugging at the horizon's roof. I am the shake and the roof
for you,
slowly finished the breeze, there is a dead brow of the sea.
Salt will be your eyes. Spite your pretty garter....

... but I have never seen a flame. Just this distance to the
                                        edge,
a slow and thoughtless taking; of life away, how I have
                                        never seen
a flame at all and yet burning in my chest is nothing yet
so to still have never seen who is this who is coming down
                                        into the ground
who is coming who is you, flat, who and though I have
                                        never seen a flame
I feel there has been a flame.
Some way over there no I don't see it I don't feel
who is this who is carried, in a barrel to the edge for me,
I have the eyes to know when I can see,
but they don't, they won't, these cancelled swells.
No, this is the circumstance,
end with us in this ground open mouthed forever staring up
like emptied teeth, there is nothing of a flame to be seen,
though we have what we need. Who is to know and see it
                                        who is coming.
A thousand enormous smiling graves and your hungry little
                                        band.

Don't cross us on the sand not heavy water salt in your
                                        tongue
cut off who comes inside the light
so much space for such a fit of weight
fall dead against the trade seas, the apparition has spoken.
I have never spoken have the eyes to see it when I see
a flame, who is coming, agitated mouth
with the eyes so she may speak. It. It. It who is so closed the
                                        beach rears up
in nightmares and folds back to the air, there's some light
but it is lifeless never speaking
or burning salt ground water
sun dizzying loss of its candour, hush.
The little apparition I find here shaking covered in the earth
and the damp; so I see who is this, who is coming; as it
                                        follows my back
for the distance and folds up, we stare and it shakes at me

in terror. How disgusting it is to stand here on the very
                                          wholesome brink.

If there's nothing to see, if to never have spoken.

then without these agitants,
the slowly killed body walks abroad
the empty scratching fields forever.
For now a dynamical imbalance, you are here
and nothing save for the ghosts of slow deaths,
who is it who stands completely still
and shows that we are here
alone they are all around, that the eyes
have decided to have never seen
a flame, to have never spoken,
and so it is, the emptied air, the beach,
the shore, the wholesome brink, your bodies,
and a tiniest pipe in the ground.

The morning is sweet the birds sing
the wires hum the tubes grumble
in the grass and the glades. You sing a happy song
you go about your world
you empty out the birds and missiles and sap...

Oh, I detest the light. And I. And I detest...
    I detest the light that is coming, and I detest
the morning and I detest the virtue and
    this thin line, so wholesome. Oh, I detest
the rivers to the sea. I believe. Oh, detest
    the laws and the motions of the tides.
I detest... I believe... in plastic. I detest,
    and I detest. You are detested. You are
detestable. Oh, how I detest... you.

*(Two people are standing on an empty stage. The lights are
bright and hard, with a sunny disposition. There is total
silence, so that when a sound is introduced there is a strange
distance to it, and that it has the quality to shock even at a
very low volume, that the distance is closer, that all that is
heard is understood.)*

– Do you remember, when you were driving in the country at night, sometimes a low thudding sound?

– What do you mean?

– A low thudding sound, sometimes, when we drove in the countryside at night.

– I remember that, yes, now you say it.

– It was strange. Sort of nice.

– What was nice about it?

– Something was happening.

– Something was happening? Is that it?

– It's something. Not like now. Now what happens?

– Pass me the tube.

– Yes.

– Great.

– I wonder what it was.

– The sound?

– Yeah. What was happening, that low thudding sound in the countryside at night.

– Weapons tests.

– Weapons tests? Honestly! You and your theories. It was probably people having fun.

– Having fun? A low thudding in the night.

– Yes. Dancing. Getting away from things.

– That's just like you.

– It was funny

– Yes it was funny

– Yes, funny, strange,

– And funny like laughing...

– It made you laugh?

– Not that.

– I could make you laugh. You wouldn't believe.

– It would ache.

– I could make you laugh. You wouldn't know,

– No.

– I don't remember. I don't care.

– We went away...

– Yes,

– And that waiter!

– Yes! Remember that waiter!
– Oh my God. Him. He could make us laugh.
– He could make you laugh.
– That waiter made us laugh.
– Funny!
– Really funny!
– Nothing better than a good laugh.
– Nothing. Nothing wrong with having a laugh.
– Fuck you.
– Really, really funny.
(the aching soil crackles. The engram flickers back to life)
– He was a good waiter. You have to be a good waiter and make people laugh. We were on our holidays. We went over to the holiday and had our dinner there every night. The waiter would come and say the specials. He always made us laugh. Ah...
– Oh Christ alive I feel destroyed. It is utterly hopeless... isn't it?
– Completely hopeless.
– Well if you can't laugh. Apparently they have this new swerving guidance system now. A modern one. It means they're harder to intercept. A type of jet. A failure. They have failures now. I failed. I felt so. I knew it. Safer.
– At least it's not like that, though. That was horrible. They were horrible.
– We're free from that.
– At least we've gone, and we're free.
– It feels amazing. Hopeless.
– I don't know...
– Yeah.
– They go up into space and then they have a varied course. It means they're harder to track. Lonely up there. In space. Imagine being all alone up there.
– Funny.
– So funny!

– ...There's bees in the meadow.
– There's a film about bees.
– A whole film?

– A great one.

– Maybe.

– Have you seen it?

– No.

– Neither have I.

– Good.

– No. Not good. I feel like I've not seen anything.

– Good.

– It's so, so horrible. What have they done.

– What have we done now.

– What have you done.

– I haven't seen it.

(Butterflies in the meadow.)

– I love butterflies. So hapless and dry.

– I'm desperate for this to stop.

– Isn't it.

– I once saw you going along the road. I saw you and I kept looking back. You were such an awful person. I could just tell. You were horrible, going

along like that and spiting me. Is it so much to ask?

– Now we're destroyed at least we can speak.

– It felt great to tell you that, to be honest. I believe in being honest. If you feel something you should say it. You should actually just say it.

– Yes.

...

(*You stare at each other, silently thinking. A butterfly lands in the empty meadow and the wires under the soil and the grass are very, very still. They think "wires". They have so many theories of wires.*)

...

– Something catalytic.

– I can remember a catalytic converter.

– Where?

– I think it was ours

– Taken. No.

– I think. I think something had to happen. I had thought it for decades. I'd lie awake at my laptop changing. Trying. Looking.

(*In the shrouded Article that is fire, long list compound of possible amendments and bills.*)

– That's just like you! Shut up. Completely hopeless. Yes... In the fire article stick your head in. You're all over the place at the moment. Mimicked meadow does my head, raining milk. Abattoirs to be forced to change its name, Yes... All over the place. Poor you. Can I help? Do you want a list?

– Don't get me started.

– It's completely hopeless, now.

– Oh, yes. I thought so. I thought of you in the flowers, in the hopeless sky etc.

– Very lyrical, flexing, in a sense.

– Flexing my muscles, because I love you.

– They wouldn't let him out. It just went that way. Shit happens.

– Things happen. These things happen. Anger, fear, in and of the meadow. Anger, the thing, the body in the belly of the wiry horrid meadow.

Drowning in the soil. Whirring surveillance. Anchor. The spider on you, officer. Shh. Be quiet, Who is this who is co-

– Shhhh.

(*A pause. The lights fade almost to nothing, then return to their bright hard sunny disposition. There is a distant agonised scream, then a further pause lasting twenty five seconds.*)

– Shall we go to the staffroom?

– There's a staffroom?

– Let's go... it's gone.

– Things just go.

– Things can't just go...

– Nevertheless, we went to the staffroom, and here it isn't.

– Gone.

– Gone.

...

(*A pause of ten seconds, then a horrible creaking sound, very close up and painfully drawn out, silence for a further five seconds*)

...

– Goney McGone Face...

...

(*Rapturous audience laughter for three seconds, suddenly cut short*)

...

– This sort of thing worries me.

– No need to be scared anymore, my sweet.

– Oh, okay... This sort of thing doesn't worry me.

– Feel better?

– Much better. Twisted asbestos.

– There's a spider on us my love, until there would be no more organ, its legs jutting from its stomach, its mane and tail flaring behind, no gambling,

...

– ...will not be still, will not sanction, will punish like a decrease.

     – No, but I will not
        be going to my sleep...

    – and I will just be going to my sleep...

Going to sleep by your side is too dangerous to live for,
when both the eyes are closed and all the tube is left
exposed; the nozzle that has made my pain is flapping like a
gorgeous mouth to taunt my mystic shadow in the meadow,
gleaming empty. No for I will not again beholden pure to
loss getting out and going back and getting out again, the
clot that walks me back along the slowness of the tube as if
you shudder back to life beneath the wirey soil pressed back
in and slip through to begin again as if it never happened
making up the movement from the underground refinery,
cause to cause to edge of loss and death you lick back up
again, once proud inside the meadow going to die there by
yourself. My practice, officer, could best be described as
moving slowly, then very quickly, then very slowly back-
wards down the tube away from my body.

...

(*A natural union between a natural man and a natural
woman in the sweet meadow. They go face to face.*)

...

– So tired….
– You'll pick up.
– What shall we eat?
– Zovirax.
– Again?
– Again and again.
– How will I trust you?
– See for yourself.
– I do.
– I know.

The lip has curled, the ant has turned, the titled switch is
                                        made in you.
Our eyes are filled with chthonic dust the same as in your
                                        mouth.
Sweat and tremble in remorse or clamp the jawline open.
Pressed inside the corner of the rotting compost data,
desperate for just one year to blink on you in kindness.
Meanwhile fourteen prophecies
whose dreams have been made up in you
a mimicry directive for planting many churches.

Every single village hall is just too deep to fill;
echoes of a life set out, but free; completely empty.
Hopelessness inside the life set out without a vision,
stretched into the partnerships of pipes
torn through our last communiqué:
Don't tell me what to do or else to let me loose and
                              smelt my speech
into the open liquid tubes, like new like love is free to
                              life.
And speech, smashed out for choice, by nought
to fuck up all the life that makes you wonder
what is left but speech made free for you to compost
                              under.
Life: The unique face the quiet tears away from you a
                              prison
made from lenience is not a fucking prison.
Prison is a punishment and not a fucking holiday.
I have seen our boys fall dead inside prison, stealing
                              life away.

– That summer, and our young love. It was false.
– My subjectivity. You asked me what it is: If there is a fire I
will not use the fire escape. It is dangerous. On the days that
I leave I walk through this city. I think about the evil that is
hovering under us.
– Have you ever stood near to The Big Pipe?
– The big pipe? They're all big pipes...
– No, The Big Pipe... The one who invisibly yawns...
– I climb through the mortar and the rain and I do not bleed
and squeeze my terrible face and I see the figures of the city
and my practice, my practice could best be described in
spit and chastity and shame and feeding routines and total
degradation and fetishistic harm to the subject, immoral
conduct in lieu of fucking my practice my practice is going
down the erratic tube at four million kHz, forgetting how to
read let alone a union, the spite I am made in the contradic-
tion at Fox & Sons the contradiction at Procter and Gamble
the contradiction at my fond memories...
– You always impressed me.

– I will show you. Gestures towards summer. Involvement
with friends in the art world. Meadow disgust. Contempt of
court. Public Order Act. I'd like to say to you this would in
the field of our dreams scream over the elastic sky, like it or
not, verbalise my dishonesty, the contradiction again in the
clarified soil, the grain, these fucking hopeless Pagans, the
regressive search for meadows, lay me down and tenderly,
artificially rip out all of my chromosomes.
– It is a closed line.
– I have closed the line.
– It is time to glue our eyes.

I can speak to you now, they said, the natural ones: I could
                              communicate
from here or from here or from here. Wherever you think.
Detergent and burned sugar.
You, you are nothing to me. The ground shakes the sky
in a clutch of those little plastic gloves they have cost / that
                              waiter
/ rains down like snowfl-/
blossom in our hair hanging like necks in the air like snow.
If you fail in this, you go late, any time from birth forward
                              to present,
and find a moment of loss or threatened loss
and fingers snapped like dead plastic
fingers, daughters, little sofffft plastic lives, hanging in the
                              plastic your
sual desire, can remember life by the Gower Pond and do
                              you slowly see.
I slowly see. It fizzes on the gantry used to love to work to
                              come inside
here every day and find a false beginning tonight as you
                              sleep ladders
will come to find myself looking forward to the new Radio
                              Times OR
articulate and shaking, post interview malaise, lily pads over
                              the pond...
that something I will never forget. No! No no no no no!
                              Today is

flattened string OR of violence / violating, residing in
the rust of its histories, emotions & ... the gangrenous
matter of
management, who now I see...meet you in the park or
the grey and empty shore
that thudd
put cuts on my face
hot plate
or bleach my crying mouth,
that way in the night thudding like fingers.
Tense and shake the bed,
mentality of lovers; gone,
gone in the shaking, disgusting, cruel,
dishonest, utterly incredible,
painfully surfaced, blurring, regressive,
blinker and radical, neuromantic,
senseless, confusing, noble and poised,
disgusting, simplistic, ghostly, monolithic,
degrading, incredible, chaste,
remiss, classified and songlike,
gluey and agitated meadow you are questioned.
When was the first time you felt humiliated?
The damaged or effective
or impossible or unusual and friendly
and classified meadow. I felt this:
I am certain the person on the other side of the gauge
galvanized steel chain link fabric fence is dead.
An actual ghost. I can see them in my mind drifting there.
That I am entirely forgotten to that moment,
even to the person who came and took me off the fence.
I felt humiliated. A great sigh heaves through the tired air
the birds chatter for a moment, and there is some relief.

Tell me about another occasion when you felt humiliated.
I was floating through the meadow.
I had just been married.
My husbands were all glaring at me. All of the families too. I
didn't knowwhat it was. My dress was torn.
I trembled in the light. They glared.

I fell down to the ground. A thread glistens in the grass near to
the woods.
It glistens horribly. Do you often feel spiteful?
Yes. Do you make bad decisions? Yes. Are you afraid to show
weakness? No. Have you ever stolen anything? Yes. Are you
not telling me something? No. Are you keeping something
from me? No. Tell me something else. It was a lazy day I was
buried up to my shins in your grave and started to cry as you
went down and the day shot into the earth, into you and I
sobbed bitterly and went with my problems and itched as the
crane lifted my neck you were there asking me this, staples in
me, injections, a big glaring light.
Did you feel like you had failed? Yes. We all fail. Do we all fail?
No. Yes, exactly, we do not all fail. Yet you felt you had failed.
Felt humiliated... Yes. I felt I had failed, felt humiliated.
Feeling like you felt you had failed and you felt humiliated
is the first step towards not thinking you thought you had failed
and that you felt humiliated. I think it went... '
Memories arrested in space...' that...
something I will never forget'...

Stepping out into the wind her nostrils flared her tail swished
her feet clattered in the wiry soil. Her hands tensed
and let loose. A maiden of the hallowed ground,
a serf of wire and tube. Her hooves to glue. Her mane to flame.
Her facial intensity. The jaundiced hungry sky
inevitably set him off, and down into the field
a man trembled in patriot fantasy,
his once giggling lips taken to incandescent
screams, far beyond reconcile and she reared up,
the gears stuttered.

There was a pub here. I love the pub.
I'm going to the pub. I'll be back soon my sweet,
and all the more, for the land!

A thread in the grass twitches
from a distance into the woods
and the E-Meter grins through the gauze.
In the cruel and heartless or effortlessly beautiful meadow a man

is walking along. In the meadow a woman is walking along.
They can see one another. How nice, to be walking
in the meadow, seeing a lovely man.
How nice to be walking in the cruel unusual
or completely lovely meadow, and there! A woman!

"Walking in a cruel meadow is like making love
to a beautiful woman," he quips in the long flowers. "What's
wrong with that?" he suddenly bellows. The cruel heart of
woman hears this bellowing man, and comes back to life,
runs after him clearing up the crisp packets and data.
His spine tingles. There is a strange thread in the grass,
she stares down at the eerie chord glistening
like a lurid hinge plate, beep, beep, beep, beep
etc. A crisp packet falls into the way, and she goes back
to the cleaning, attends to the meadow.
Just then a crow bellows, for rain.
They meet, naturally, and agree to have sex
with one another. Oh good. She lies down in the blades
of his ire, does her best not to set him off.
"Europe. Northern. White. Baltic." he snarls...

– Having sex with you is a bit like making love to a beauti-
ful woman. Connected to a damp feeling. The population.
You know, before they had all this...
– Shh. Just try to be happy.
(*He pulls a piece of tape across his mouth and makes him-
self go to prison*).
...
And so it was that she wandered alone in the damaged
meadow, mending the seams of reality, gently and quietly,
like any corrupted monad. Bollocks to you, she dares to
think, and turns off the path into the woods.
These were the woods of a terrified child. But in the summer
it is only a quiet hazard. She trips along through the sticks
and bracken.
There is no birdsong. It is extremely quiet.
She runs back into the meadow. She speaks to him again.
He is irate.

– Remember that waiter? Wasn't he funny!
(*He is glaring like stone.*)
– That waiter was funny wasn't he.
She kicks the ground with her foot and notices that just
below the earth there are thousands of wires and tubes.
One of the tubes she sees has an enormous clot of blood
in it. They are going to make us extinct. That wai-... They
meet every year in a secret location. They all do. They are.
It is unclear who is speaking. They scream about the sky.
The wires are under the ground. I don't like parachutists.
He was funny. He was funny! He was funny, wasn't it? He
has to have been funny or I can no longer speak. I will have
to die. Is there anything else?. No, not any more, he was
funny wa-... I don't want to go alone into the woods....

And oh the day away,

What's the worst thing you're capable of?

...

It is a very strange world, like the old one, only closer. Where are you. The meadow. The tube. The flute. You walk again into the woods and go near to a tree. You peel back the bark and begin to think about looking underneath it. You have a look, and under the bark of the tree is, surprise surprise, tubes. Eighty different tubes. You knew it. He knew it. He told you, so you knew it. Tubes. Wires. Windows on the World. He knew it. He told you. You should have known. They made love. They fucked like wires and tubes. You walk further into the wood. The climate whispers to the trees. Thank you. No, thank you. The desperate boiling wires are thrashing under your feet. You go on, into the woods, into the face of return. You walk along for minutes and minutes. What is that smell? And then you are halted. You can hear the screaming of a man in the meadow. It is intolerable. You knew this all along, so you went to the wood and walked calmly along until you were halted. Suspended just above the ground, your arms tensed against the strain of the silk. You struggle and are caught in torsion. The irate man in the meadow such a long way away. Dying alone in his furious peace. You hang in the web, disgusted, appalled, shuddering. And then you are eaten by an enormous horrible spider.

Acknowledgements

Sections, drafts and fragments of *Hopelessness* have been published in Erotoplasty, Tentacular, The Earthbound Poetry Series, Poetry Wales and Senna Hoy. A French translation of the book is forthcoming from Même pas L'hiver. Part of the composition of the text was financially supported by No Matter who commissioned a performance of the work and published an early manifestation of the last section of the book. My thanks to them and to the editors of the publications listed above.